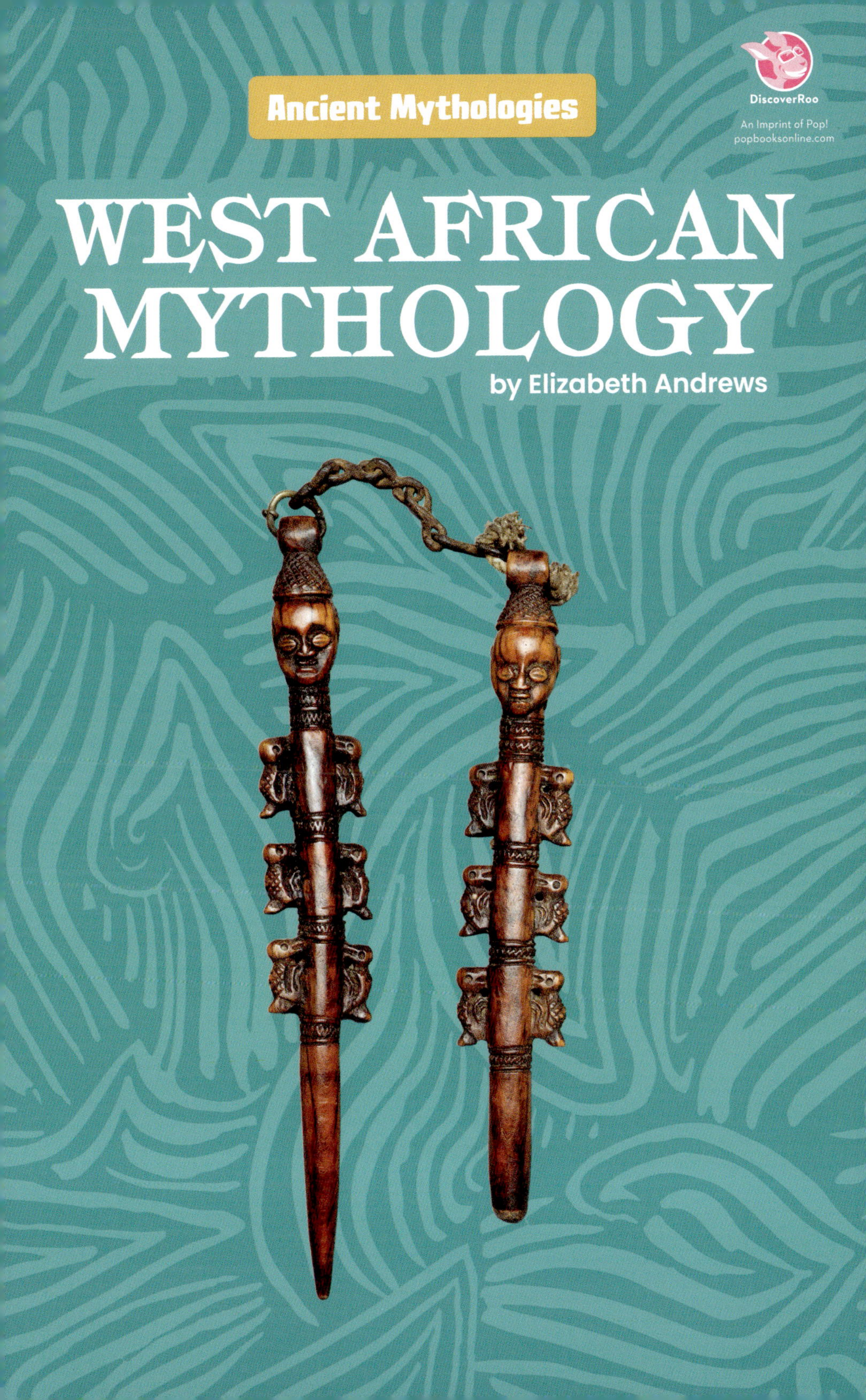
Ancient Mythologies
DiscoverRoo
An Imprint of Pop!
popbooksonline.com
WEST AFRICAN MYTHOLOGY
by Elizabeth Andrews

WELCOME TO DiscoverRoo!

This book is filled with videos, puzzles, games, and more! Scan the QR codes* while you read, or visit the website below to make this book pop.

popbooksonline.com/african-myth

abdobooks.com

Published by Pop!, a division of ABDO, PO Box 398166, Minneapolis, Minnesota 55439.

Printed in the United States of America, North Mankato, Minnesota.

102024
012025

Cover Photo: Shutterstock Images

Interior Photos: Alamy Stock Photo, Shutterstock Images, Getty Images, Rodrigo Tetsuo Argenton/Museu Afro Brasil/Wikimedia Commons, Brooklyn Museum/Wikimedia Commons, Collectie Wereldmuseum (v/h Tropenmuseum), part of the National Museum of World Cultures/Wikimedia Commons, Yeniajayiii/Wikimedia Commons, Wellcome Images/Wikimedia Commons

Editor: Krissy Sterling

Series Designer: Colleen McLaren

Library of Congress Control Number: 2024938632

Publisher's Cataloging-in-Publication Data

Names: Andrews, Elizabeth, author.

Title: West African mythology / by Elizabeth Andrews

Description: Minneapolis, Minnesota : Pop!, 2025 | Series: Ancient mythologies | Includes online resources and index

Identifiers: ISBN 9781098247072 (lib. bdg.) | ISBN 9781098247638 (ebook)

Subjects: LCSH: Mythology--Juvenile literature. | Mythology, West African--Juvenile literature. | Gods, African--Juvenile literature. | Deities--Juvenile literature. | African mythology--Juvenile literature.

Classification: DDC 299.62--dc23

*Scanning QR codes requires a web-enabled smart device with a QR code reader app and a camera.

TABLE OF CONTENTS

CHAPTER 1

CREATION MYTH

Before humans came to be, the earth was a watery wasteland with endless sky above. Olorun, the chief god, had created the earth. He lived in the sky with other **deities**. The sky was so close to the earth that some deities climbed down spiderweb bridges to visit.

WATCH A VIDEO HERE!

One time, Olorun called the deity Obatala to him. He sent Obatala down to earth with a snail shell filled with dirt, a pigeon, and a hen. Olorun ordered him to spread the dirt and create land on the watery waste.

Olorun has no constant human or animal form. He is also called Olofin and Olodumare.

Obatala sprinkled the dirt from the shell. He put down the pigeon and the hen. The **Sacred** Drummer played his music, and the earth shook. The birds spread the dirt. Solid ground formed.

DID YOU KNOW?

The story of Obatala would have been told while a drummer played a beat.

Obatala returned to Olorun when he thought the job was done. Olorun sent Chameleon to inspect the work. When Chameleon returned, it told Olorun that the land was wide but not dry enough for earthly beings to stand on. Obatala went back to finish the job.

Some stories say Obatala came down to earth on a golden chain.

The West African god of the drum is called Àyàn.

After four days of work, Chameleon found the land to be firm enough. Obatala planted trees so any being would have supplies to live. Then Olorun ordered Obatala to make humans from dirt. Olorun breathed life into the molds. These molds became the first humans.

Nearly every society has a creation myth. The myth of Olorun comes from the West African Yoruba tribe. Myths are stories that often involve deities and **supernatural** events. They are not always based on facts. Myths helped people make sense of the world around them.

CHAPTER 2

ORIṢHA

The Yoruba tribe has the most well-documented mythology in West Africa. Usually, tribes shared the stories of their **deities** and legends through spoken stories. Very little has been recorded. The myths were shared during important **rituals** in communities.

LEARN MORE HERE!

The Yoruba people call their deities orisha. There are hundreds of orisha. Olorun created most of them before humans existed. Later, some Yoruba **ancestors** were made into orisha after having a large impact on their people. Orisha have the power to move between the spirit world and the earth.

Shango was a Yoruba king who was made into an orisha.

West African Tribes

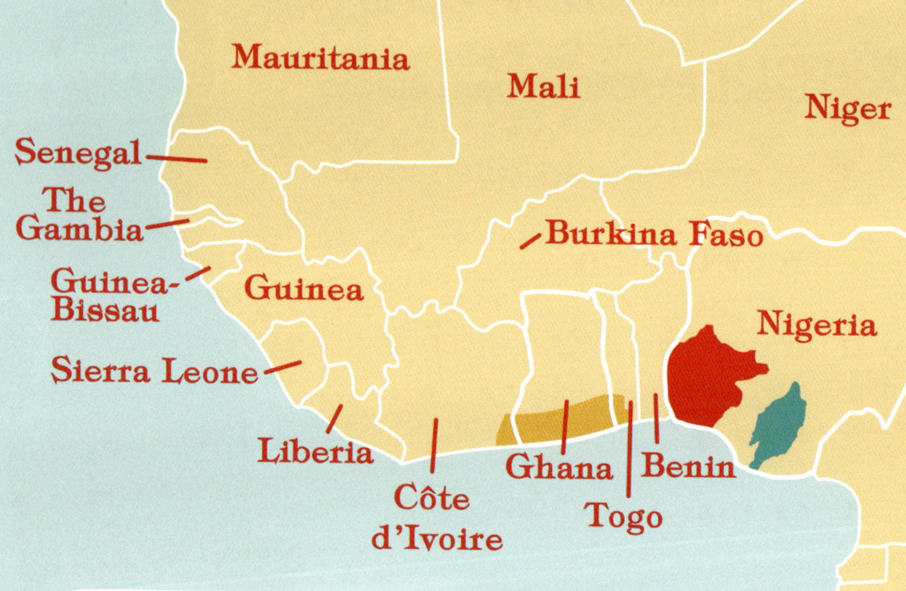

Key

Akan tribe land

Yoruba tribe land

Igbo tribe land

West Africa is filled with rainforests, savannas, and dry land. Ancient people lived mostly in small villages and were closely connected to their families. Tribal land was not divided by countries. Country borders were created by European **colonizers** in the late 1800s.

Orunmila is one of the most important orisha. He is second in command to Olorun. He is the deity of wisdom and **divination**. Orunmila was the only witness when Olorun created the world. Orunmila helps humans solve their problems.

BABALAWO

Babalawos are Yoruba spiritual leaders. They have a close relationship with Orunmila. Babalawos are knowledgeable about Yoruba and orisha history. During rituals, Babalawos share messages from Orunmila. They get these messages by throwing seeds or nuts upon a divination tray. Orunmila is more likely to answer Babalawos if their trays are beautiful. They are also healers and make medicine for their tribe members.

Babalawos keep their materials in ritual containers.

At first, orisha were all equal in Olorun's eyes. Before they had their own powers, they spoke with Olorun and Orunmila about any issues or ideas. The orisha believed it would be easier to keep the world going if they all had their own powers.

Olorun and Orunmila decided to pour all powers down from the sky.

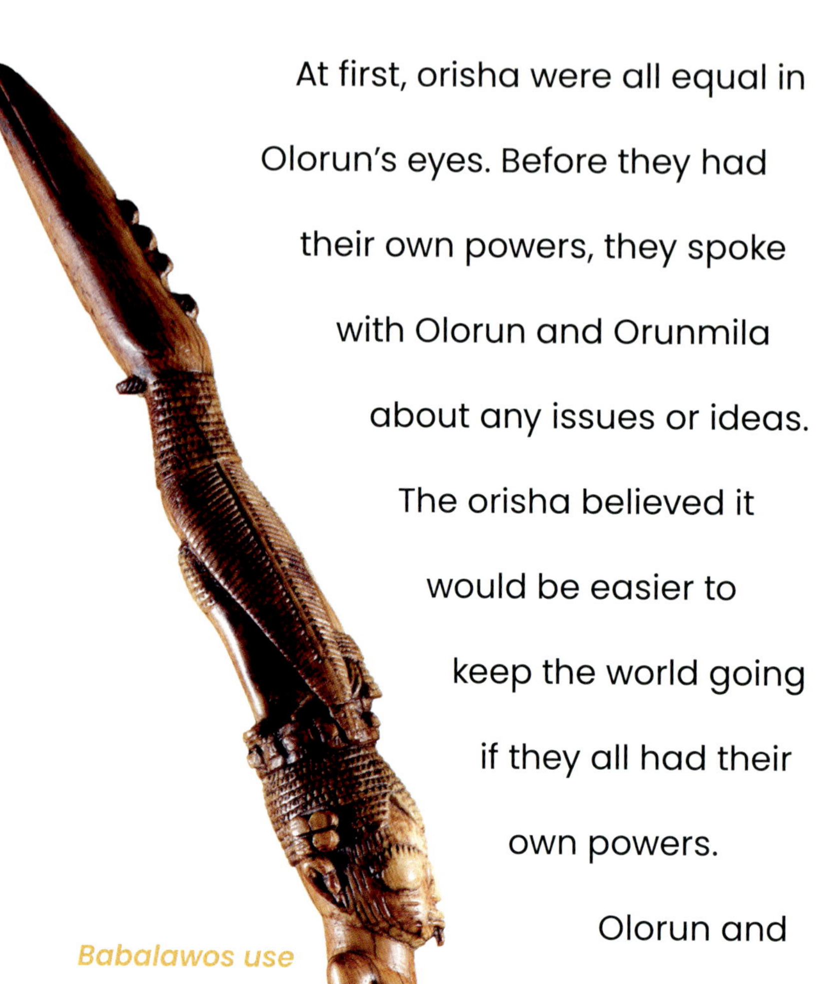

Babalawos use long tapping sticks to contact Orunmila during rituals.

Chickens were often sacrificed to certain orisha for their favors.

Whatever powers an orisha collected were theirs. Some orisha were faster and stronger than others. They collected the most impressive powers.

CHAPTER 3

WATER STORIES

Myths from West Africa often explain why things happen in nature. Oshun is the Yoruba orisha of **fertility**, love, and fresh water. She is the youngest orisha. Oshun sends floods and droughts to people who fail to honor her and the land. She also sends rain and clean water when humans are in need.

EXPLORE LINKS HERE!

Weather is often dry in West Africa. People ask deities to bring rain.

DID YOU KNOW?

Oya is the orisha of wind, lightning, and storms. Obatala is her father.

The Osun-Osogbo Sacred Grove is located in southern Nigeria.

In one story, all the orisha stopped listening to Olorun. He got angry and took rains away from the earth. The drought was difficult. The orisha apologized, but Olorun was too far away to hear. Oshun was brave and decided to fly to Olorun in the form of a peacock.

It was a difficult flight. When Oshun got to Olorun, most of her feathers were gone. She looked like a vulture. Olorun was surprised by her **sacrifice** and sent the rains back. Vultures are still sacred to the Yoruba people today.

People who worship Oshun may carry fans similar to the one shown in this statue.

The Igbo people believe in a water spirit named Mami Wata. She is often shown with a mermaid tail or wrapped in snakes. Mami Wata represents health and good fortune. She also represents dangers. Some stories say Mami Wata steals humans when

Mami Wata can control snakes.

Mami Wata is well-known for her beauty.

they are in bodies of water. She drags them to her world underwater. When they return, they are often healthier and wealthier.

CHAPTER 4

TRICKSTERS

Trickster stories are very popular in mythologies. Tricksters are often underdogs who are not expected to win in struggles. But tricksters win by using their smarts, not their physical abilities. Anansi is a famous West African trickster character from the Akan people.

COMPLETE AN ACTIVITY HERE!

Nyame, Akan's sky god, is similar to Olorun. They are both all-knowing and watch humans from the heavens.

DID YOU KNOW?

Anansi is the son of the Akan's sky god.

In one myth, Anansi and his son were struggling through a drought. His son got help from the king's **jester** to bring the rains back. Anansi tried to go to the jester too. But he accidentally killed him. The king punished Anansi and ordered him to carry around the jester's body forever. But Anansi tricked an ant into carrying it instead. This myth explains why ants can carry such heavy things.

Anansi usually takes the form of a spider.

Anansi tricked the sky god into giving him all of his stories.

Eshu is the trickster orisha of the Yoruba people. He guards the door between the spiritual world and the human world. Any messages people want to send to Olorun or an orisha must go through Eshu. Eshu must be honored during all **rituals**. If he isn't, whatever requests or prayers humans want to send to the spiritual world are lost.

Eshu understands every language on earth.

West Africans use a lot of yams, plantains, and beans in their meals.

Eshu is clever. His tricks are planned carefully. Once, Eshu embarrassed Olorun. He told Olorun some orisha were planning to steal from his garden that night. When night came, Eshu took Olorun's shoes and walked through the garden. He stole yams.

Today, people may ask the orisha for strength.

When Olorun woke up, he saw that his yams were stolen. He ordered all the orisha to compare their footprints to those left in the dirt. When no one's footprints matched, Eshu suggested they compare Olorun's. Sure enough, the footprints matched. Olorun was so embarrassed that he left for the sky and never came back to earth.

West African mythology has become more well-known. Today, some people honor orisha and participate in celebrations much like their **ancestors** did. Ancient mythology is a great way to understand what communities cared about in the past.

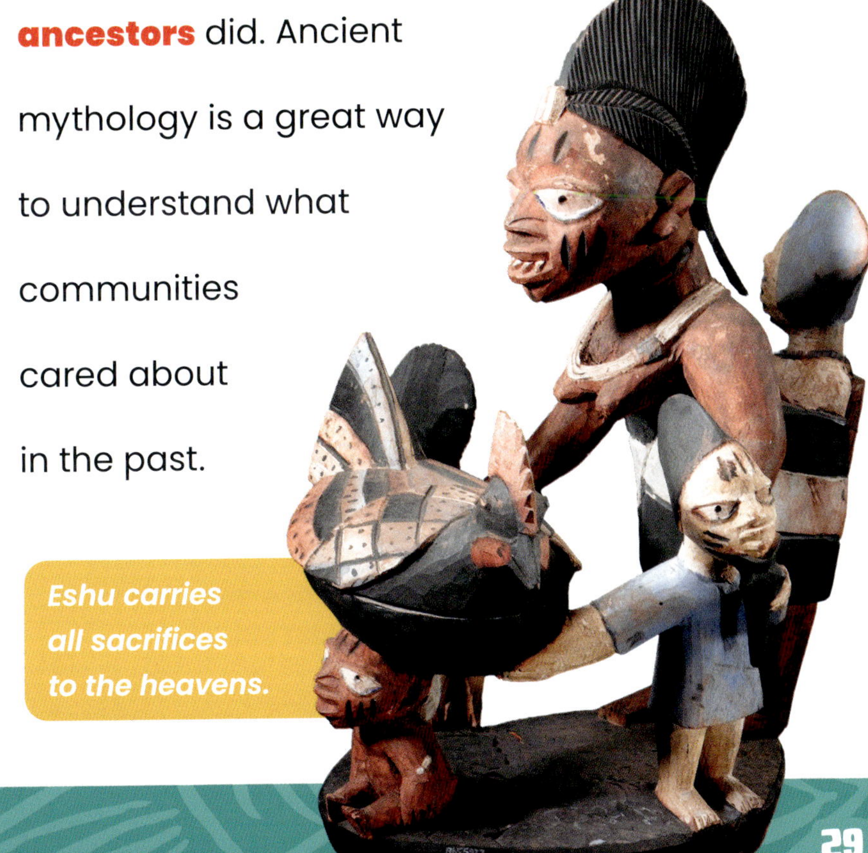

Eshu carries all sacrifices to the heavens.

MAKING CONNECTIONS

TEXT-TO-SELF

If you lived at the time of the ancient Yoruba, which orisha do you think you would have prayed to? Please explain your answer.

TEXT-TO-TEXT

Have you read any other books about ancient mythologies? If so, what did those mythologies have in common with West African myths?

TEXT-TO-WORLD

West African deities such as Oshun and Mami Wata were very important to ancient people. With the help of an adult, look up water deities from other ancient mythologies. Write a few sentences about the similarities and differences you see between them and Oshun or Mami Wata.

GLOSSARY

ancestor — a family member from an earlier time.

colonizer — a person who takes control of an area or a country that is not their own, especially using force.

deity — a god or goddess.

divination — an art or practice that seeks to connect with supernatural powers to receive information.

fertility — a woman's ability to have children.

jester — a person kept by powerful people to provide entertainment.

ritual — a spiritual action performed in a certain way.

sacred — something connected with worship of a god.

sacrifice — a person or animal killed as an offering to please a god.

supernatural — having to do with forces beyond what is natural.

INDEX

This book is filled with videos, puzzles, games, and more! Scan the QR codes* while you read, or visit the website below to make this book pop.

popbooksonline.com/african-myth

*Scanning QR codes requires a web-enabled smart device with a QR code reader app and a camera.